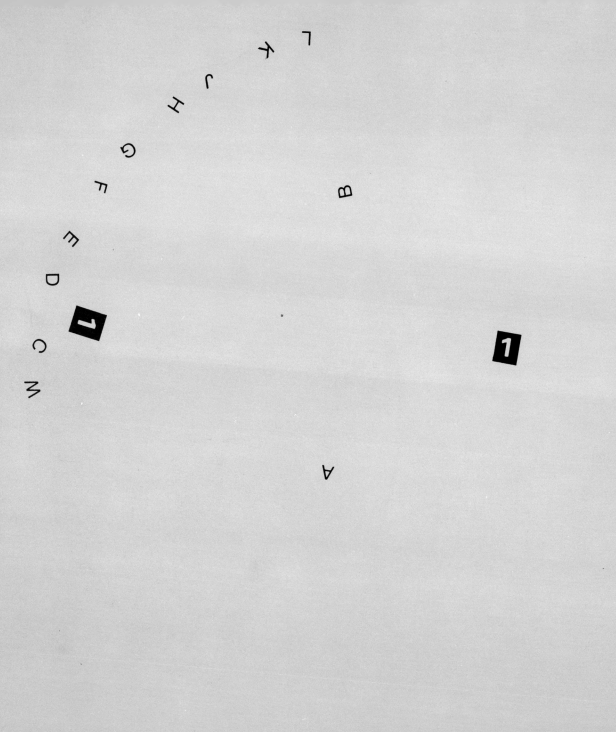

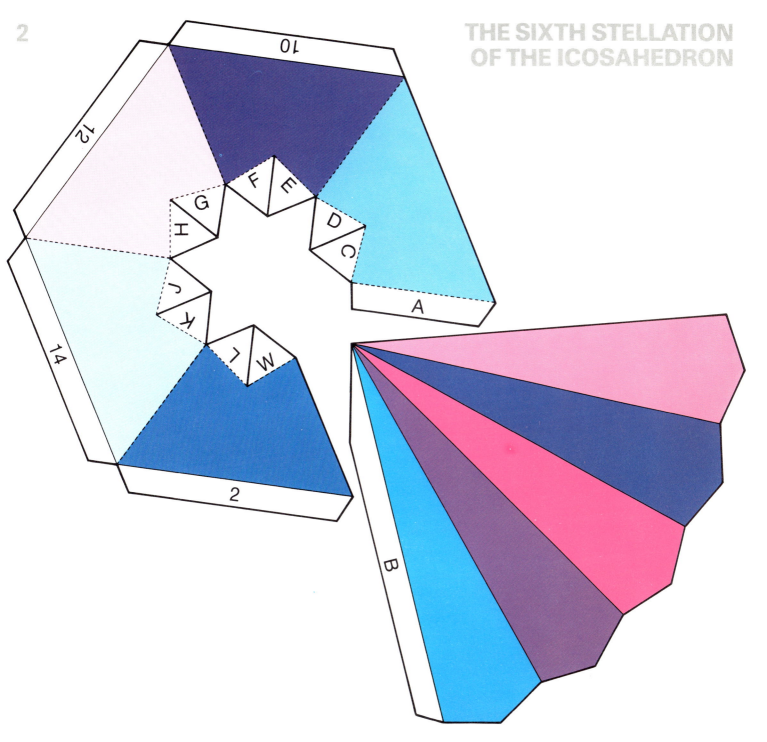

THE SIXTH STELLATION OF THE ICOSAHEDRON

THE SIXTH STELLATION OF THE ICOSAHEDRON

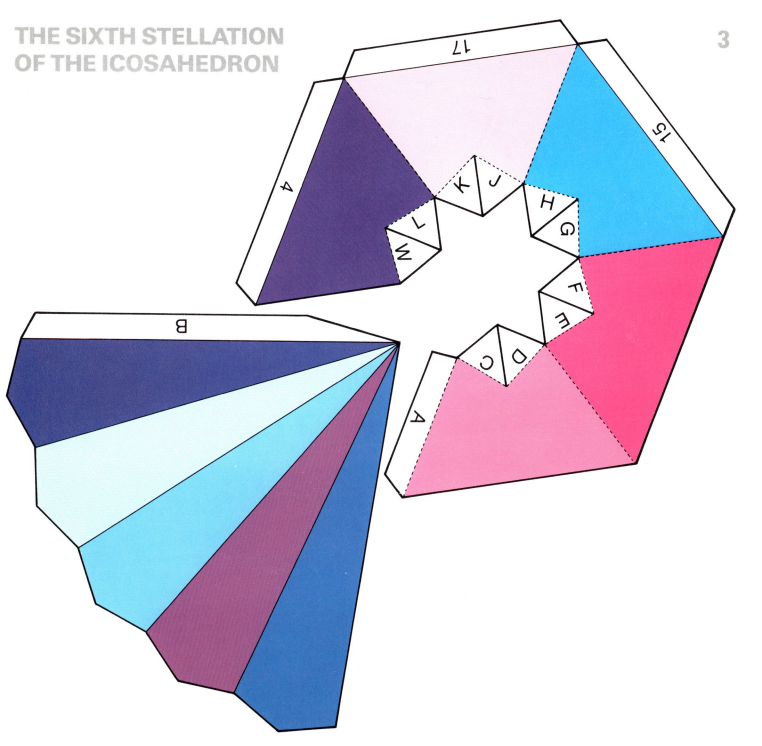

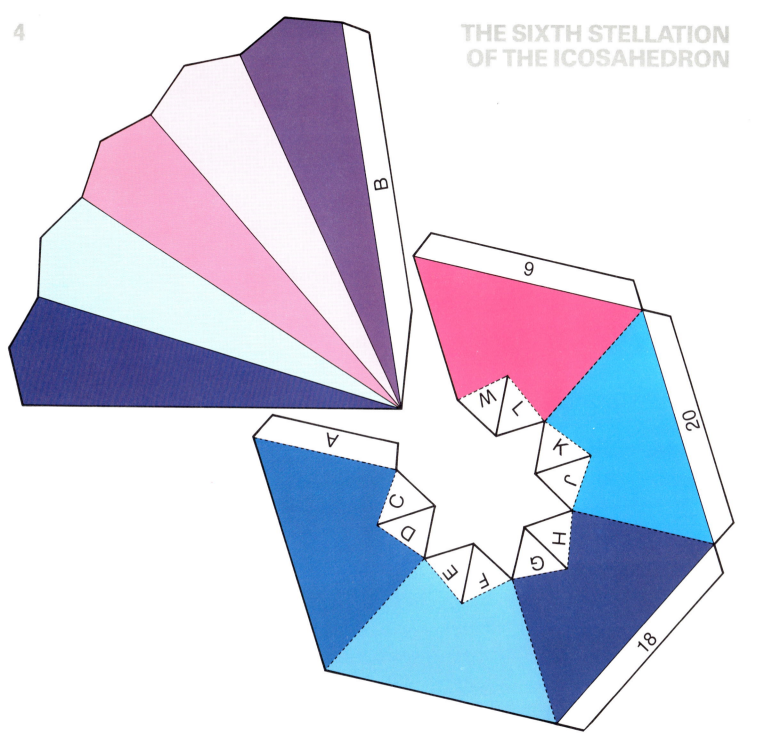

THE SIXTH STELLATION OF THE ICOSAHEDRON

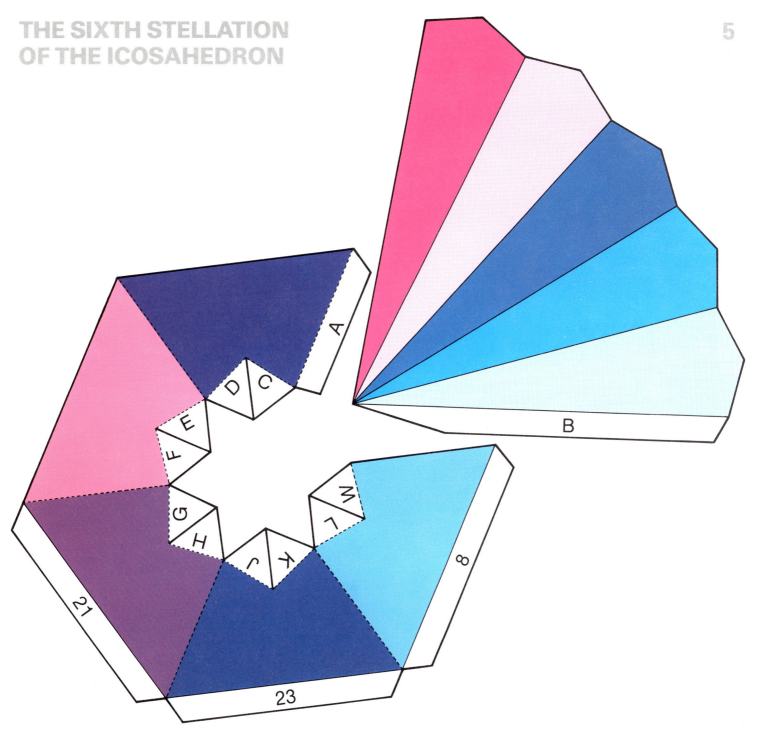

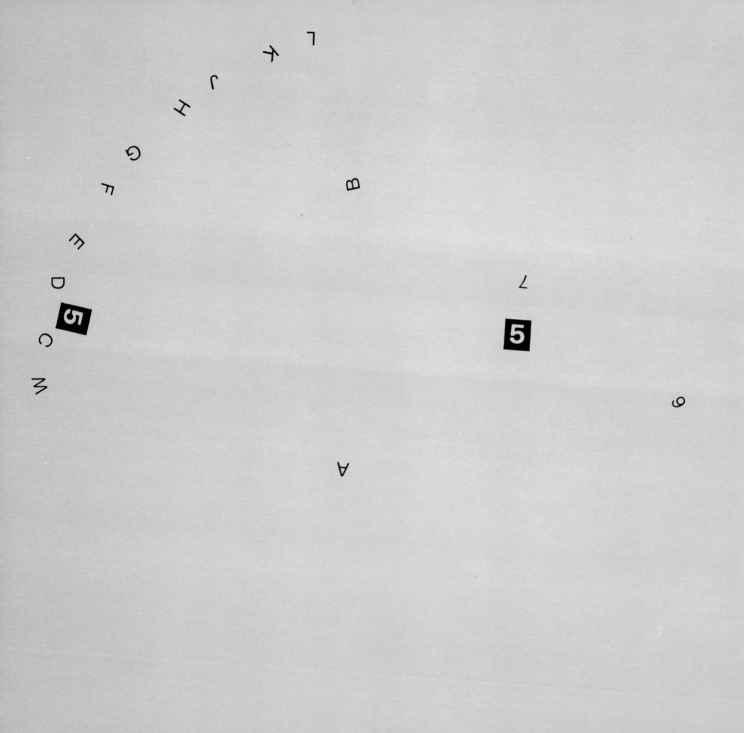

THE SIXTH STELLATION OF THE ICOSAHEDRON

THE SIXTH STELLATION OF THE ICOSAHEDRON

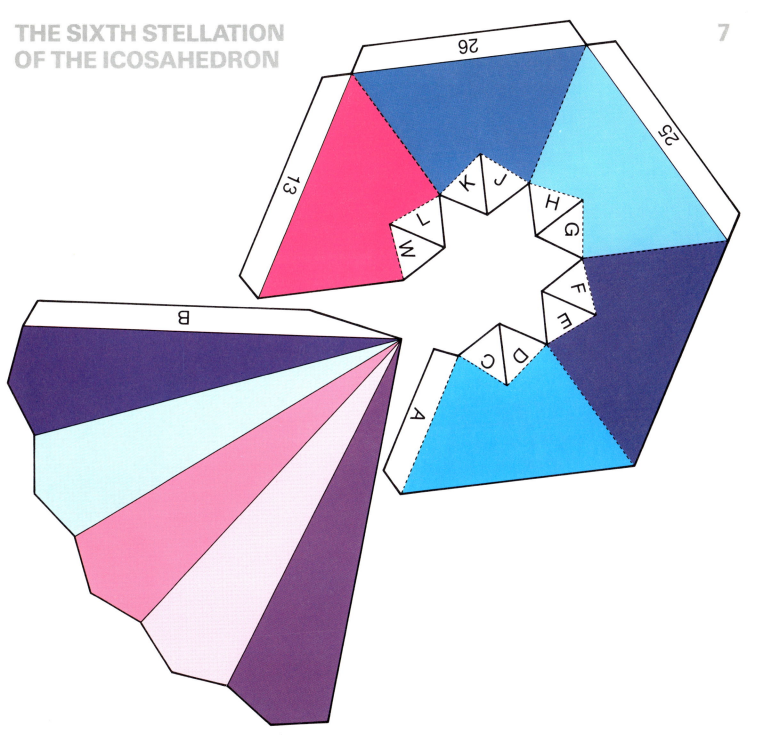

A

11

7
12

7
M
C
D
E
F
G
H
J
K
L
B

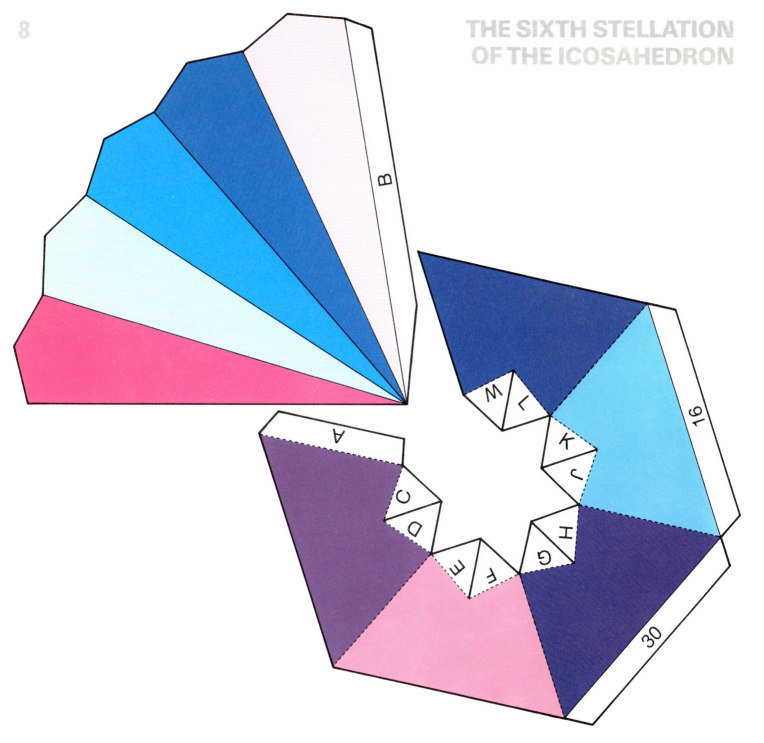

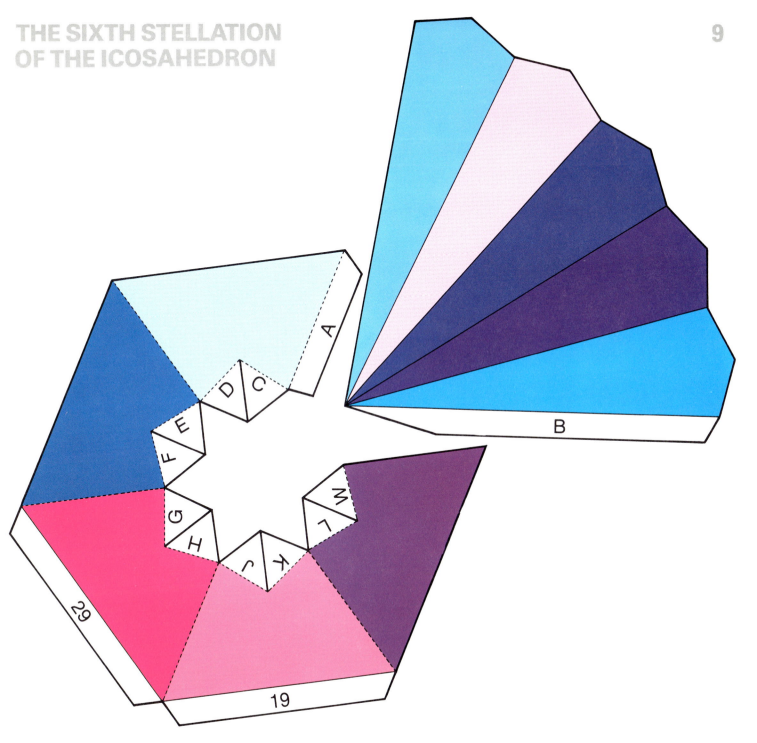

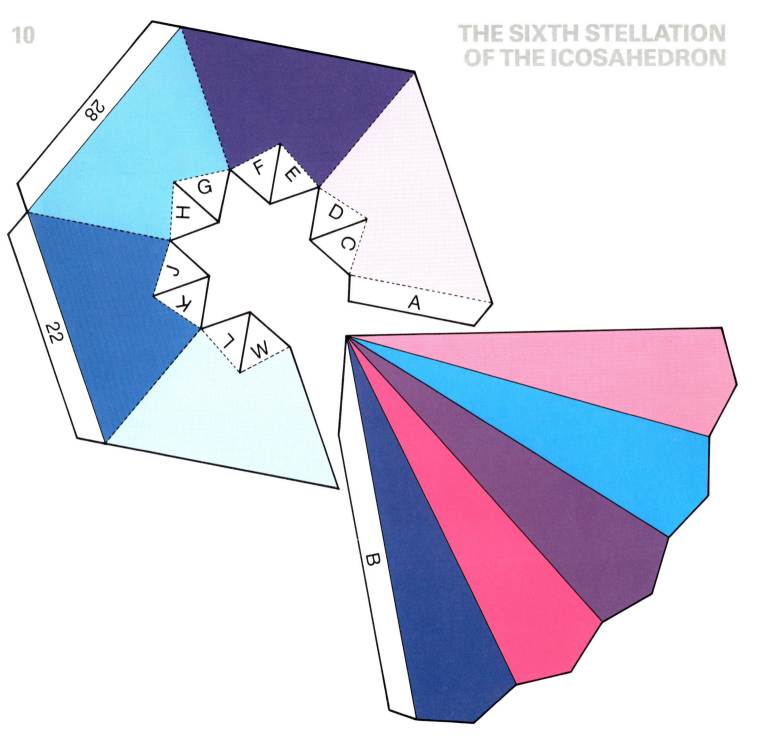

THE SIXTH STELLATION OF THE ICOSAHEDRON

25

24

A

22

11

23

11

B

C
D
E
F
G
H
I
J
K

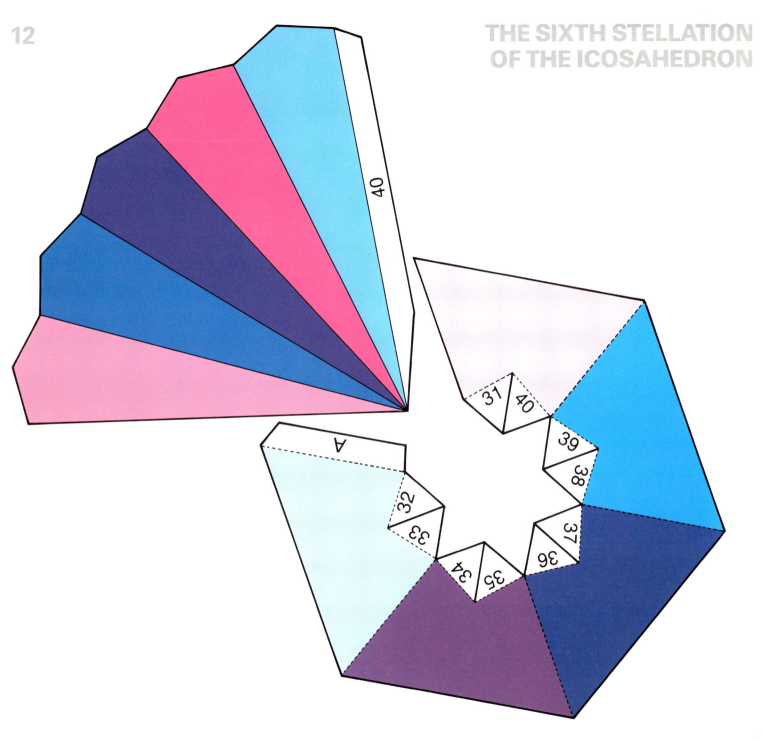
THE SIXTH STELLATION OF THE ICOSAHEDRON

12